Animal Wisdoms

Messages to ignite the soul

JULIA VAN DER SLUYS

Copyright © 2024

All rights reserved. This book or any portion thereof may not be reproduced or used in any manner whatsoever without the express written permission of the author except for the use of brief quotations in a book review.

Printed in Australia
First Printing, 2024
ISBN: 978-1-7636899-1-6
White Light Publishing
www.whitelightuniversal.com.au

About this book

I have designed this book to be a handy pocket best friend from the Animal Kingdom… and Tex!! You will find my recently sleeping pooches 'Texinisms' scattered throughout this book with his wise and fun wisdom, in honour of him – he was always my little spiritual side kick in life, so it is no wonder that he has continued on the tradition over the veil. His zest for life was inspirational and I hope you enjoy these messages he has to share, just a heads up, he loves balls!

You will find many different animals in here that wanted to come through with some timely messages. Some are in our lifetime, others are mythical, some you may need to google to see what they look like as they were quite specific! Either way they have some beautiful messages to share with you all, so enjoy and soak up their amazing words.

Read it how you will, there is no right or wrong way to do it. I personally like closing my eyes and asking 'What message do I need to read today' then I open to a page and devour the words. Letting them sink in, letting them fill my heart and soul up with magic. You can then choose to go about your day with their words whispering in your ear, filling you high vibe cup up, or you may like to journal what it brings up for you, means to you, inspires you to do.

Again, there is no right or wrong, just what is perfectly right for you.

Till next time…
keep walking your spiritual path xx

GUPPY

Let your colour and flair run wild today. Show your inner rainbow.

Sparkle sparkle sparkle.

JACK RUSSELL

You could feel either way today - like you are pogo-ing pogo-ing pogo-ing with no chance of getting off or you may need to put a bit of pep in your step. You'll know instantly which one you are.

Be like us, constant energiser energy ready to burn, ready to take leaps and bounds.

Go balls to the wall and take a superman leap. Don't worry about the fall! Just do it and always expect to either land on your feet, or something will cushion your fall.

GREAT DANE

It doesn't matter about the length of life or situation but about the quality of it. You could live to be 100, yet hardly of truly lived at all. Yet someone could go out with a bang at 20 and had lived three lifetimes full in that same time. It is up to you to lead a fulfilling life in whatever way that means to you. Excuses are just those. So today make sure it is as rich and full as you want

KIWI

Snuffling through leaf matter... scratching out some grub... we are what we are, what we are. Kooky and unique. Strange and amazing... we are what we are, what we are.

GLASS LIZARD

We get mistaken for snakes all the time but really - what is in a name? We are not here to live up to a name or a preconceived notion of who and what we are meant to be. We just are! None of that matters in our world... and it shouldn't in yours.

Just be, today.

GLOW WORM

I WISH I WAS A GLOW WORM A GLOW WORMS NEVER GLUM COS HOW CAN YOU BE GRUMPY WHEN THE SUN SHINES OUT YOUR BUM. YOU MAY NOT HAVE A LITERAL GLOW BUM, BUT YOU STILL HAVE THAT BEAUTIFUL RAY OF LIGHT THAT SHINES SO BEAUTIFULLY OUT OF YOU. LET IT KEEP A SMILE ON YOUR DIAL, TURN YOUR FROWN UPSIDE DOWN AND MAKE SOMEONE ELSE SMILE WITH DELIGHT TOO. YOU ALWAYS HAVE IT IN YOU!

CURLY COATED RETRIEVER

Be your own best friend, your own loyal companion. Rely on you to make you smile. Be there for yourself in a way that no one can and in a way anyone can. It is time, so timely that you become your own biggest fan.

GIBBON

Take a leap of faith today! Knowing there is a net of safety provided by the universe to catch you. Stop hiding behind the leaves and just go for it!!

GREAT WHITE SHARK

Are you using all your senses and the greatness these can give you? Are you the mighty shark in your field or are you playing at skittish crab?

Be the great white shark in your world.

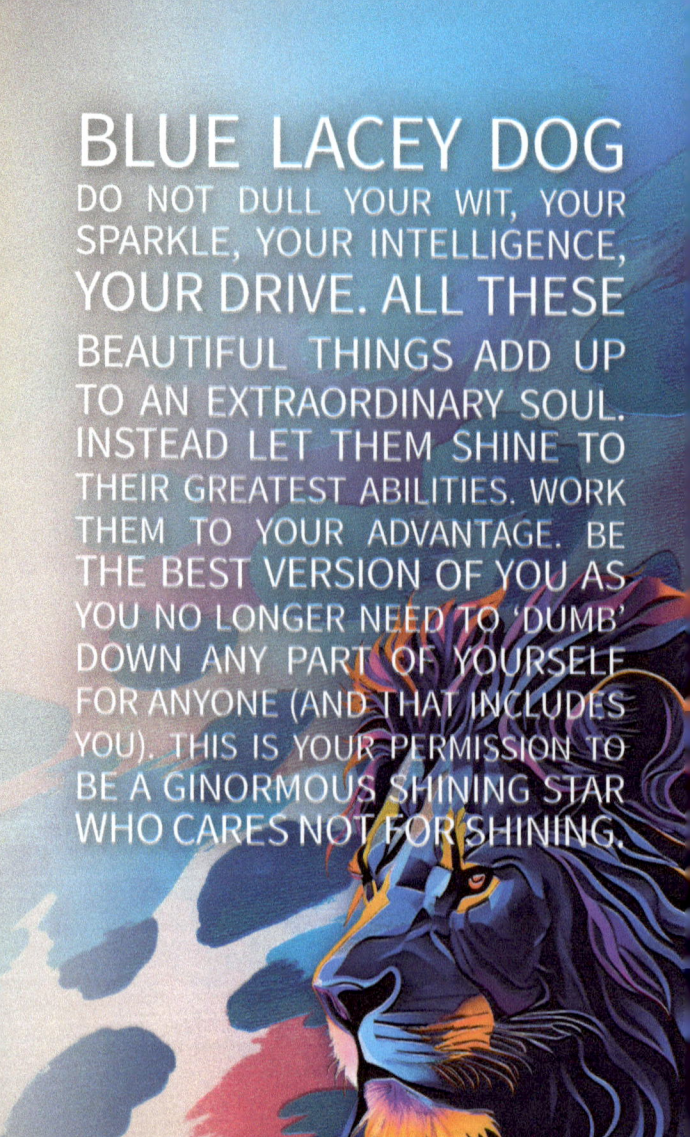

BLUE LACEY DOG

DO NOT DULL YOUR WIT, YOUR SPARKLE, YOUR INTELLIGENCE, YOUR DRIVE. ALL THESE BEAUTIFUL THINGS ADD UP TO AN EXTRAORDINARY SOUL. INSTEAD LET THEM SHINE TO THEIR GREATEST ABILITIES. WORK THEM TO YOUR ADVANTAGE. BE THE BEST VERSION OF YOU AS YOU NO LONGER NEED TO 'DUMB' DOWN ANY PART OF YOURSELF FOR ANYONE (AND THAT INCLUDES YOU). THIS IS YOUR PERMISSION TO BE A GINORMOUS SHINING STAR WHO CARES NOT FOR SHINING.

Tiger Salamander

Here's looking at you!

It is so easy to get bogged down in the everyday monotony. To just keep on keeping on. Today break the norm in your day! Doesn't matter how small or big, do something to put a crink in the link of same old same old.

GALAPAGOS PENGUIN

What do you want to do? Like seriously what would you like to do? With no ifs, buts, umms. Sit down with yourself and get very clear on what you want to do. Then stand tall and do it! No matter the odds, time, money space - if it is meant you will find a way.

NIGHTINGALE

Fly like it could be your last. Sing like it is the last time it may happen. Breathe like there's only so many left – this makes you love and appreciate life to the extreme. To make memories rather than merely existing.

GHARIAL

Same same, but different. Really that's all humans are. But it's that difference that truly makes you YOU. Sure, what you consist and parts you are made up of are relatively the same but your small differences, your soul make you so uniquely you. So instead of putting those uniqueness's down - celebrate them! Worship them! Take out a newspaper spread about them! Roll in the deliciousness that is YOU!!

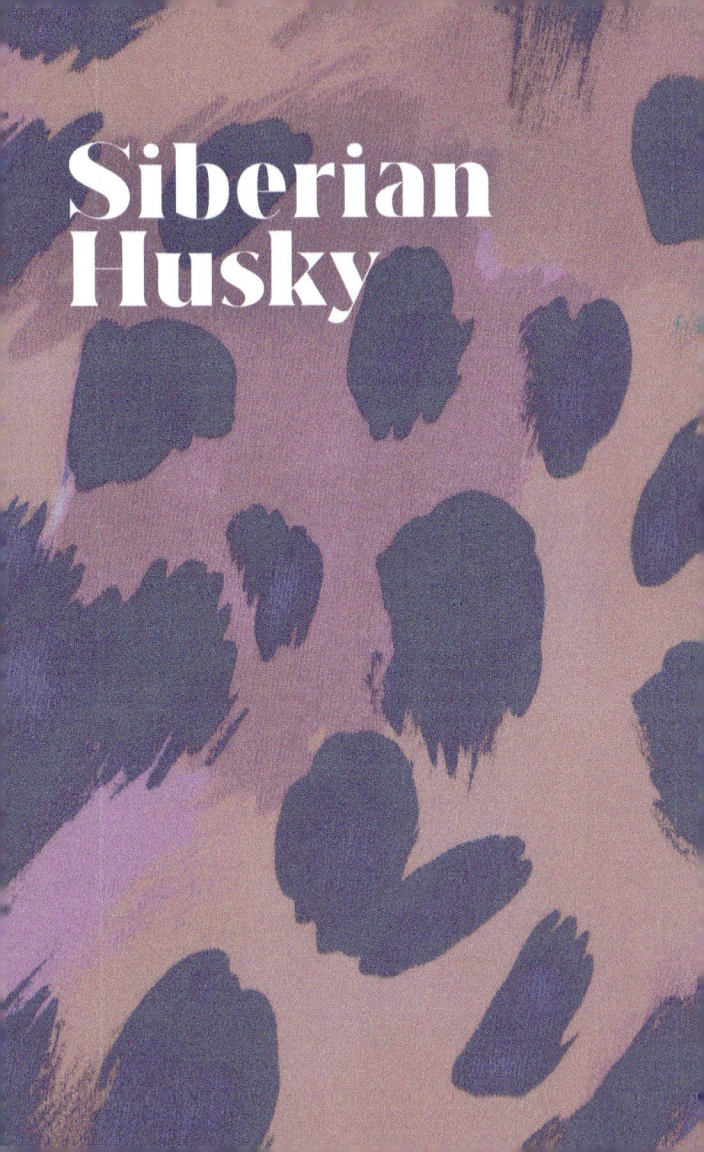
Siberian Husky

Be aware of your surroundings but still have an explicit trust that all is ok and well. Let your instincts guide you to the right paths and choices. Let your warm coat warm you from the inside out.

MOOSE

These boots were made for walking... get a little exercise today... or maybe there is something that needs to be booted out of your life today... whatever it may be or what you choose to do with your boots today - do it with lightness and positivity. As they say honey is better than vinegar. Or however it goes!

JELLY FISH

Being translucent does have its benefits! Is there any areas of your life where you can let go a little, where you can talk a bit more about? Do a little bit more. You may think you are being open - but maybe something needs to be said or done directly to get the message across.

GERMAN SHEPHERD

Protect your energy today, in whatever way you need to do that. It could be to take some downtime away from others, it could be to 'suit up' when you step out of the house to keep your energy all to yourself and not bring in others.

Fishing Cat

Scoop whatever you would like out of life today.

It is up to you what you scoop - remember you can always throw it back in if it is something you do not want. You are the chooser of your day... and destiny!

BUMBLE BEE

SIP THE BEAUTIFUL NECTAR OF LIFE TODAY. EMBRACE ALL THE JOY AND LIGHT THAT THE DAY HAS TO OFFER. WHETHER YOU ARE BUZZING AROUND BUSY OR ABLE TO PERCH AND SIT AWHILE, ENJOY THE BEAUTY OF THE DAY.

TEXINISMS

Spread your love infectiously. Let the world have no way but to fall in love with you!!

CANTELOPE

Run through the fields of change and allow your feet to take you where you need to go. Just go with the flow and watch the world unfold for you.

`This animal chose to come through with this name, the glimpse I saw of the animal would remind you of an Antelope or similar.

DRAGONFLY

Flitting from place to place allows you to discover all that you love or not as the case may be. Enjoy new discoveries today even if you discover that it is something that you may not enjoy or ever want to do again. There are always positive lessons.

SHETLAND PONY

We may be small, but we be fierce. Where can you be fierce? Where you can be a gladiator wrapped in a cuddly cute package? It cannot always be sunshine and mud pies, sometimes you need to stand tall and strong and slay what needs to be done.

HULIENDI

Walk through that doorway.
Allow transformation, rejuvenation, opportunities to explode all around you in delightful colours and sounds. Enjoy the juicy feeling of being exactly where you are meant to be.

The body of a horse with long flowing dark hair, a breathtaking feeling of light and love seems to emanate from Huliendi - touching all that think of her.

Bask in the sunshine. Glory in your pack. Relax and allow yourself utter stillness today. In stillness can come the most profound.

WASP

Stings when needing to protect oneself. Are you stinging to protect yourself from danger, or because it has become armour and the norm for you? Today dive deep in your armour and see what can be switched. You do not need to keep that stinger out at all times.

CONCAN

Nothing can stay the same. So, enjoy the changes, embrace the difference and go with it. Life is not meant to be stagnant.

Think colourful like the toucan, with the ability to fly and swim.

Concan is a mythical creature with monkey like features.

BROWN BEAR

Childlike wonder, long naps, using nature to survive, gentle lumbering yet powerful stance. Life of bear can be extraordinary. What can you take from us today.

LILIANT

Stand in your power today.
Close your eyes and ask to access that innate power, that candle flicker inside of you. Feel the peace and serenity that comes from connecting with your soul. Ask if it has anything it wants to say to you. Allow the dragons fire to cleanse you of anything that no longer serves you.

Liliant is a mix of Dragon and horse with a beautiful long mane with the face of a dragon. Liliant is a mythical animal that chose to come forward today.

WILD HOG

DO SOMETHING WILD AND IMPULSIVE TODAY. LEARN TO SNIFF OUT OPPORTUNITIES. LEARN TO ZIGZAG YOUR WAY THROUGH YOUR CHORES. LEARN WHEN TO RUN AND WHEN TO TURN AROUND AND RUN STRAIGHT AT SOMETHING.

APHID

How precious that we get to feed and build our shelters on beautiful plants and trees. How indulgent that we get to sip the nectar of life from these. You also have the ability to 'sip' on the nectar of life, to indulge in the beauty of nature. Are you?

TEXINISMS

You're here to see me?? Hells Yeah!! Expect and know people are here for you! Act like it, know it, bask in it. Roll and wag that tail and know that you are the beez kneez. Sometimes it totally can be all about you and it's a good thing! Make friends with everyone. Cows, horses, people – it's all the same baby – just make more friends!

MEERKAT

Be observant today. Yet have fun. We can enjoy our moments yet know instantly when we need to be aware of something. It is a skill that you too can learn. Being in the moment helps.

HARLEQUIN

**There's an echo all around -
can you hear it?**

If you are willing to listen imagine the greatness you could hear, the magical, the laughs. Listen today. This also begs that if your own words used were to be echoed back to you, how colourful would they make your life? Would it be drab blacks, browns - lower energy vibes or would it be colours of the rainbow pulsing in heavenly energy?

`Harlequin wished not to be seen but reminded me of the wise echo/voice that you hear. Harlequin feels ever changing and unique.

COUGAR

STRATEGY. LEARNING TO PUT INTO MOTION THAT WHICH YOU WANT MOST OUT OF LIFE. WHAT IS STOPPING YOU. ACT LIKE THAT IS NOT THERE, PUSH THROUGH IT AND GO FOR GOLD. ONLY YOU IS WHAT IS TRULY STOPPING YOU, ALL ELSE CAN BE MAS-TERED AND CHANGED.

Fox

You can adapt to any surroundings.

You have a wily cunning mind if you choose to use it. Think outside the box and the answers will come to you.

DOLPHIN

Dive into the ocean of joy! Spring into love. Everything is what you make it. So, it is up to you to make your ocean full of calm peaceful water or rough and choppy.

KOALA

Today conserve your energy for what you truly want. Don't waste it on meaningless stuff today. Soft and cuddly wins the day but remember the claws if you need them. Eucalyptus oil will be a winner today… of course.

GNAT

Whittling your way slowly through things can sometimes be the way to go. Not always but sometimes. Sometimes those ideas or thoughts need to percolate before being introduced to the world. The darkness can provide answers if you light the candle enough for you to see them. There is nothing to fear there.

Being the fastest doesn't always mean coming first. There is a skill to knowing when to run flat tack or to slink our way to victory. Pay attention to what way works for you today.

PTERODACTYL

You have the capability of 'flying' above things when they get too hard difficult etc. This doesn't mean putting your head in the sand but it means stepping back from an observational viewpoint and not allowing it to hit you full force. It means being the better person and rising above it all. It also means you can dive the hell down and grab what you're after with both hands.

IGUANA

THIRD EYE! DID YOU KNOW WE LITERALLY HAVE A THIRD EYE THAT CAN PERCEIVE BRIGHTNESS? FUNNILY ENOUGH YOUR 'THIRD EYE' IS ALSO BRIGHTNESS AND ALL SPIRITUAL YUMMINESS. IT CAN BE THE MOST AMAZING TOOL FOR YOU, IF YOU KEEP EXERCISING IT JUST LIKE YOU WOULD ANY OTHER MUSCLE. TODAY SIT AND FEEL YOUR THIRD EYE. YOU MAY GET A TINGLING OR STRANGE SENSATION, OR YOU MAY FEEL ZIP. BUT BRINGING YOUR AWARENESS THERE GIVES YOURSELF A GREEN LIGHT TO START USING IT. OH YEAH AND EVEN BETTER IF YOU DO THIS WHILE RELAXIN' IN THE SUN... COS HEY WHAT'S A DAY WITHOUT SOAKING SOME OF DEM RAYS.

TEXINISMS

Be the biggest brightest YOU!! that you can be. Doesn't mean you have to be like me and be the biggest personality in the room. But don't hide you. Don't erect walls that people can't see to the real you. Let it all out to shine!

HORSE

We stand tall and proud with our owner. Becoming one. Happy to work as they do. Feeling what is needed and being strong enough to go on. Today reflect on all that has been and gone. Give thanks for the life you lead. Give thanks to those that have come before us.

VULTURE
SOMETIMES
IT IS NECESSARY TO EAT AWAY AT THE 'DEAD' OR 'ROTTING' PARTS OF YOU. TO ALLOW REGENERATION TO OCCUR. THERE IS NOTHING TO FEAR, IT IS A NATURAL PROCESS WE ALL MUST TAKE.

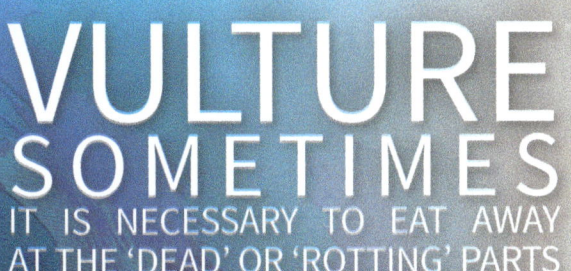

TEXINISMS

Leave them feeling happy.

ELEPHANT

Stand tall and strong. Allow yourself to have our memory. Hug your tribe, your pack - both blood and chosen as ferociously in love as we do.

HUMPBACK WHALE

NOT EVERYTHING NEEDS TO BE SPOKEN - SOMETIMES THE BEST THINGS CAN BE SAID THROUGH ACTIONS, FEELINGS AND VIBRATIONS. REMEMBER YOU CAN MOVE THROUGH ANYTHING WITH GRACE - LOOK AT US! GIANTS OF THE SEA YET SMOOTH AND GRACEFUL AS CAN BE.

Deer

Celebrate your delicateness today.

Sit in your feminine energy of love, strength and light and know these make you strong beyond belief.

ALBATROSS

Deftly flying across the ocean - wind in our wings, salt air in our midst. Deep diving to get tasty morsels that give us life. Where can you deep dive today? Imagine if you cannot get to the beach the feeling.

TICK

Sometimes it is necessary to burrow under the skin. Sometimes you need that life blood to know which way to go in life. Today there may be an area in your life that needs you to burrow under to know which way to take/what to do etc. Spend a little hibernation time with yourself today.

FINCH

Flitter through life rejoicing. Hooraying the greatness. Celebrating the trials. Twittering your love of life. Knowing when to move on to the next thing.

We can patiently wait for hours waiting for a snack and we can jump into motion in a heartbeat. Today something needs either your patience or action. You will know what it is.

TREX

WHILE WE HAVE PHYSICALLY LEFT THIS EARTH - OUR LEGACY LIVES ON. WE WILL NEVER BE FORGOTTEN. TODAY THINK ABOUT WHAT LEGACY YOU WANT TO LEAVE.

STORK

Deliver yourself good news today! And remember you can travel near and far in your daydreams. There is no limit there, only what you put on yourself. Today be limitless.

SLUG

You can always find a way to move forward if you truly want to. Look at us with just a body yet we thrive and get by in truly amazing ways. Today have a good look at where you are wanting to go and do that. No ifs or buts about it. Strengthen the 'muscles' you have and need to use to do this successfully.

ROBIN

Spread good cheer and sparkliness everywhere today. Most especially to yourself. Give yourself a high five over every task you complete. Make life a celebration today. Wear your heart on the outside so the loving rays can be felt and seen. Rejoice in life.

TEXINISMS

Ball, ball, ball, ball - Do a cherished thing EVERY DAY, don't leave it too late to enjoy what you love doing. Doing what you love increases your good vibes and makes the day much more easily managed.
So, what you makes you smile or your most favourite things in the world to do? Incorporate a few mins into your day, just to stop and do something that you absolutely love to do.

SLOTH

MOVE WITH UNHURRIED MOVEMENT TODAY. BE PRECISE AND PRESENT WITH EVERYTHING YOU DO. SLOW AND INTENTIONAL WILL GET YOU FAR TODAY.

MOLE

Sometimes you don't need to see where to go. Just trust that you are going in the right direction.

Echidna

Today thank your prickly bits for keeping you safe. That is their job after all.

Just remember beyond those prickly bits - there is the beautiful soft fluffy centre that is open and loving.

JITTERBUG

Do not fear our name! Having the jitters isn't all bad. You may have the jitters today. Something not quite feeling right, a sense of needing to move but a bit clueless on where too. Maybe a feeling of lost or increased emotions. You have the power to control these though - in whatever way they show for you. Direct your energy to something that helps them - write it out, ask what you're feeling to talk to you, do movement of any kind to shake it out. You'll be directed to what you need to do if you allow.

WOODPECKER

Constantly knocking on your goals, little by little, day by day will bring them to fruition. It doesn't matter how little or how long it takes to get there - just that you kept keeping on. Don't be worried about bothering others. You just keep on your path. Knock knock knocking on.

CUTTLEFISH

WE HAVE SO MANY USES THAT SOMETIMES WE ARE NOT EVEN AWARE OF OURSELVES. WE ARE SIMPLY QUITE AMAZING. IF YOU NEED HELP SEEING YOUR AMAZINGNESS - PERHAPS IT IS TIME TO ASK THOSE AROUND YOU WHAT THEY THINK ARE YOUR GOOD QUALITIES - YOU MAY JUST BE SURPRISED. IF YOU DON'T WANT TO ASK SOMEONE, ASK THE UNIVERSE, THEY'LL LET YOU KNOW.

PIG

The simple things in life is what we enjoy every day - any food that is given to us. Any mud we get to roll around in. Any company we get to enjoy. Today think and be grateful for the simple pleasures in your life. For they are simply the greatest.

Home is wherever you scent mark.

Revel in your home, which also includes your body – for that is what is housing your soul. Allow yourself to roll around in the magic that is your home, your life. Pounce on fun and laughter today.

FIREFLY

When darkness falls - there we are with our tail so bright. Lighting up the night with magic alright. You can be that light, it does not need to be physical. It goes for daylight too. You may not need to see it but it is there guiding our way all the same.
Be magical.

CABOOSE

Be ready for the unexpected. Life can change at any time and it is better to roll with it than fight against it. You can turn anything your way if you are willing. Be willing today. Be open today.

TEXINISMS

Get mad, then get happy. If you feel a certain way, go ahead and feel it. Once you felt it, literally get happy. Getting happy means dropping that other emotion other than happiness – quickly like a hot potato or a tennis ball you want thrown.

GIRAFFE

Allow your long neck to see above what is happening in your life - so you can see from a different perspective, look at it in a different way to what you normally may. You do not need to rush today - go with a gentle Grace and ease, unhurried just as we do. All of those branches you thought you couldn't reach - you can today.
Reach for the stars.

GOANNA

FEEL THE WARMTH ON YOUR FACE AND BODY AS THE SUN FILLS YOU WITH ITS VIBRANT, LIFE GIVING ENERGY. LET IT FLOW THROUGH YOU, TO ALL PARTS OF YOUR BEING - MAKING YOU FEEL ALIVE AND WARMED BY THE VERY ESSENCE OF LIFE. GOLDEN LIGHT PENETRATING EVERY SINGLE CELL. BASK IN THE LIGHT OF THE SUN.

GOLDFISH

Such Beautiful colours. Such joy in receiving food, such fun in discovering our home each and every day. Notice how we never get bored of the same thing over and over again? You can also feel this way as you give yourself permission to feel the 'new' in your life. It doesn't have to be new to feel renewed.
Be humble and enjoy.

Beetle

While our outer shell may look hard and impenetrable - look again.

While it is hard and protects us, it is also fluid and moving. It is important to have boundaries, but it is also important that those boundaries aren't made into unmoving walls that you hide behind. Today choose to have strong boundaries that give you freedom to move.

CHICKEN HAWK

Set your sights on something today and really go for it. It doesn't matter the trees you have to move past, the grass you need to see through. Keep your eye on the prize and you will succeed.

HEN

Cluckity cluck Cluckity cluck. The mother in you wants out! The nurturing earth femininity. Today nurture is the key word. Not just for others but for yourself. Self-care is so important. So is scratching beyond the surface to find the hidden gold underneath.

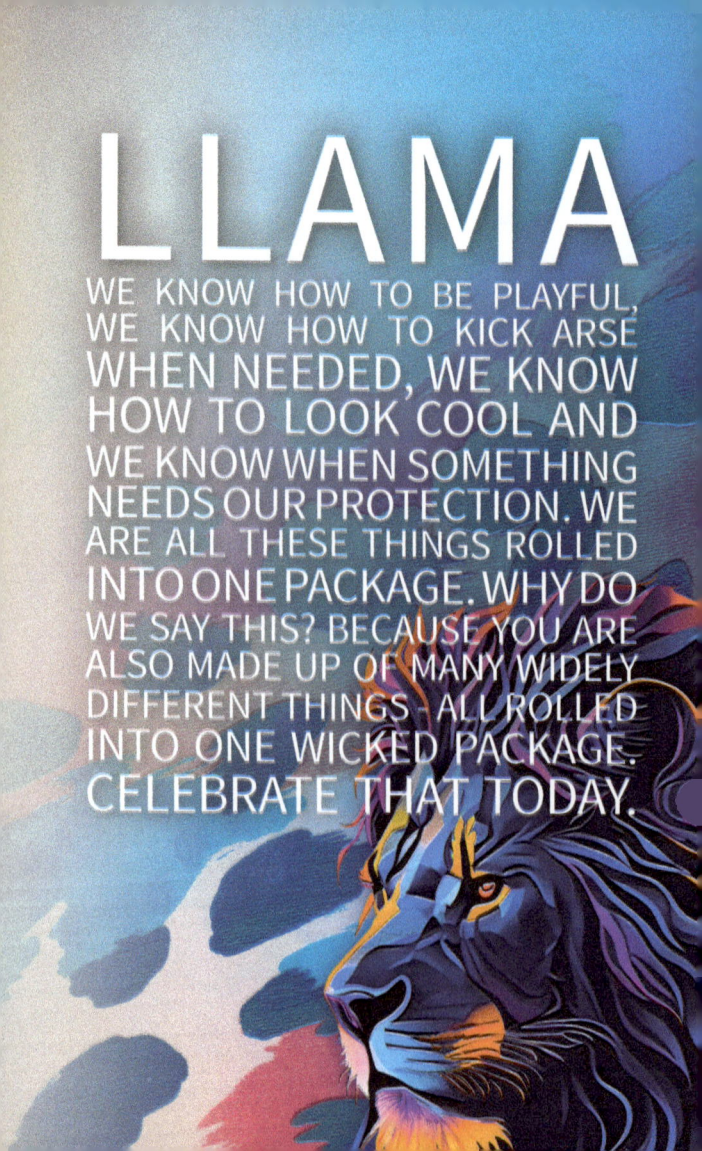

LLAMA

WE KNOW HOW TO BE PLAYFUL, WE KNOW HOW TO KICK ARSE WHEN NEEDED, WE KNOW HOW TO LOOK COOL AND WE KNOW WHEN SOMETHING NEEDS OUR PROTECTION. WE ARE ALL THESE THINGS ROLLED INTO ONE PACKAGE. WHY DO WE SAY THIS? BECAUSE YOU ARE ALSO MADE UP OF MANY WIDELY DIFFERENT THINGS - ALL ROLLED INTO ONE WICKED PACKAGE. CELEBRATE THAT TODAY.

TEXINISMS

Show up every day and NEVER give up!

CENTIPEDE

You may not have physically a million legs like we do - but you still have the power in you to use a million legs like we do. To slink along merrily using all that is available to you. What are you not using enough of? Today vow to do something with that part of you that may be feeling a little neglected.

Owl

Oh wise one! For you are wise! Go through life today looking through your wiseness - imagine it like wise glasses. That allows you to see and learn everything you need to in any moment of the day. Hoot your way through today by asking yourself what you really want to do today. And do that!

Hooting good tides to you.

WORM

The early bird catches the worm. But there are many worms so perhaps you catch the right worm at the right timing for you.

Today don't be worried about woulda/shoulda/coulda, instead relish where you are right now. You're in the perfect spot to see that worm. Dig deep today, the worm has no problems being in the dark. It is there to support and nourish you.

So embrace with warm loving arms.

SPIDER

YOU ARE ETERNAL. SO, DON'T FRET THE SMALL STUFF. INSTEAD FOCUS ON THE JOY OF BEING IN THIS BODY, RIGHT HERE, RIGHT NOW. THERE IS TIME FOR EVERYTHING. LEARN TO USE ALL OF YOUR 'LEGS'. DEVELOP AND USE ALL OF YOUR MUSCLES THAT YOU ARE CAPABLE OF. USE ALL OF YOUR MAGIC AND DIVINE - DON'T JUST LET IT LIVE INSIDE YOU. GLARE THE WORLD WITH IT.

MOTH

Be drawn to the light as we are. No matter the darkness - we can always find a spark of light, always. Find the light in your every day. Be the light. Imagine you have the same beautiful dust that covers our wings and know it makes you magical. For you are magic.

HORSE

Can you feel that beautiful breeze through your mane? The freedom? The joy?
Today choose to feel freedom no matter what the circumstances. We like having purpose/ a job to do - so give yourself a purpose today.

TEXINISMS

Get mad, get happy – for a dog this is super easy, for a human with too much thinking? Not so much. So, choose something you can do – a ritual, a saying, a doing action that means you're 'dropping it like it's hot' and getting on with the biz of being happy. Do this particular thing only when you're ready to let go and get back to happy so your body, mind and soul will remember it as such and act accordingly.

OTTER

Ride the Rapids, Glide with them as if you are one. See how smoother the ride is when you go with the flow and not struggle against the tide? Today go with the flow.

SNAIL

Your home, your safe place is wherever you are, and where you need it to be. Because it is you! Learn to use it wisely to protect yourself, to empower you and make you stronger. Learn to dance in the puddles with joy. Let your inner child out to splash about when the 'weather' is unpleasant - they can always find something to enjoy. And finally let your senses guide you, we are all about the senses!

SHEEP

THERE ARE TIMES TO BE INSULATED WITH YOUR WOOLLY DELIGHT AND THERE ARE TIMES TO BE BRAVE AND STEP FORWARD, SHORN AND WITH NOWHERE TO HIDE. BE BRAVE IN THIS VULNERABILITY. THIS IS YOU!!!

TEXINISMS

Be so full of beans, your tail curls.

GULL

Everything is gold! Everything is magic! Everything is food! Check over anything and everything to see if it could be something that could be used in your life. Some people see rubbish - but we always check as it may hold gold for us. Be determined. We never give up until we check for ourselves. Be the loud one, be the one barging your way through... or be the one at the back, knowing you will get a crumb when the time is right - whatever way calls to you - do that! Work from instinct.

Stand tall and proud. Preen your mane. Sometimes all you need to do is stand strong to be majestic, you do not need to prove anything. Do not let fear touch you today. If you feel an inkling - ask on your own majestic lion to help you bravely face it. To own it and step through it. Bravely go into the unknown, the wild.

KANGAROO

Bounce, bounce, bounce - bounce your way through life with Joy and Enthusiasm in everything that you do, from the most mundane task to the most thrilling. Life has a way of lightening when you do this, and everything begins to feel joyful no matter what you are doing. Hold your nearest and dearest close to your heart, in the warmth of your pouch. Accept them and watch magic happen.

Goanna

Emotions can be heightened today, you may feel unsure of all that is popping up.

Be present, feel and then release into Mother Earth with love and gratitude. You do not need to carry the weight of the world on your shoulders. By sitting still - we can find great wisdom and catch flies.

CRAB

Sideways scuttles are just what they are. They are not going backwards but they always reach their destination. They know when to bask in the sun and when to hide in the shadows. None of this is hiding in fear, it is simply knowing when there could be a predator or not. Today celebrate your side scuttles, your basking and hiding. All of it is ok.

BILLY GOAT

ENJOY LIFE. ENJOY THE PROCESS OF EACH DAY. FIND THE JOY AND GRATITUDE IN EVERY SINGLE LITTLE TASK. FEEL VICTORIOUS WHEN YOU 'CLIMB THE MOUNTAIN' OF EACH TO DO AND STAMP YOUR FEET AND PUFF YOUR CHEST WITH PRIDE. FIND JOY IN EATING ANYTHING THAT YOU CHOOSE TO EAT - YOU KNOW US GOATS LIKE TO EAT!!

BILBY

Step quietly through nature as you learn to live and grow with it. She is your friend, your deepest confidence - treat her as such. Learn to let go among the trees, share your emotions with the ground, tilt your head to the rising sun and feel the warmth on your face. Leave her as you left her and be grateful for her, as there would be no life without her.

RAM

Ram knows when it is the time to butt heads and when it is time to retreat gracefully. Knowing the retreat is done with ease and a knowing deep inside, it is not tucking your tail between your legs, it is simply a retreat. Be the ram in your kingdom and lead from your intuition, your grace and flow. Be attuned to your cycles so you may carry out your day to day with ease. Stand strong and tall.

ANT

Realising that you must check into everything that comes into your path - is this right for me do I want it, will it make me happy. By asking these kinds of questions to everything that comes your way - you don't lose opportunities or grasp at stuff you do not need. Having help can make the workload lighter.

BLACK COCKATOO

The time is nigh to ride the high winds in your life and not let the small stuff below you get you down. Let your broad wings open and soar, let your voice be heard and remember to have fun and be social along the way. Life is more fun when there is more than one, be it in human or animal form.

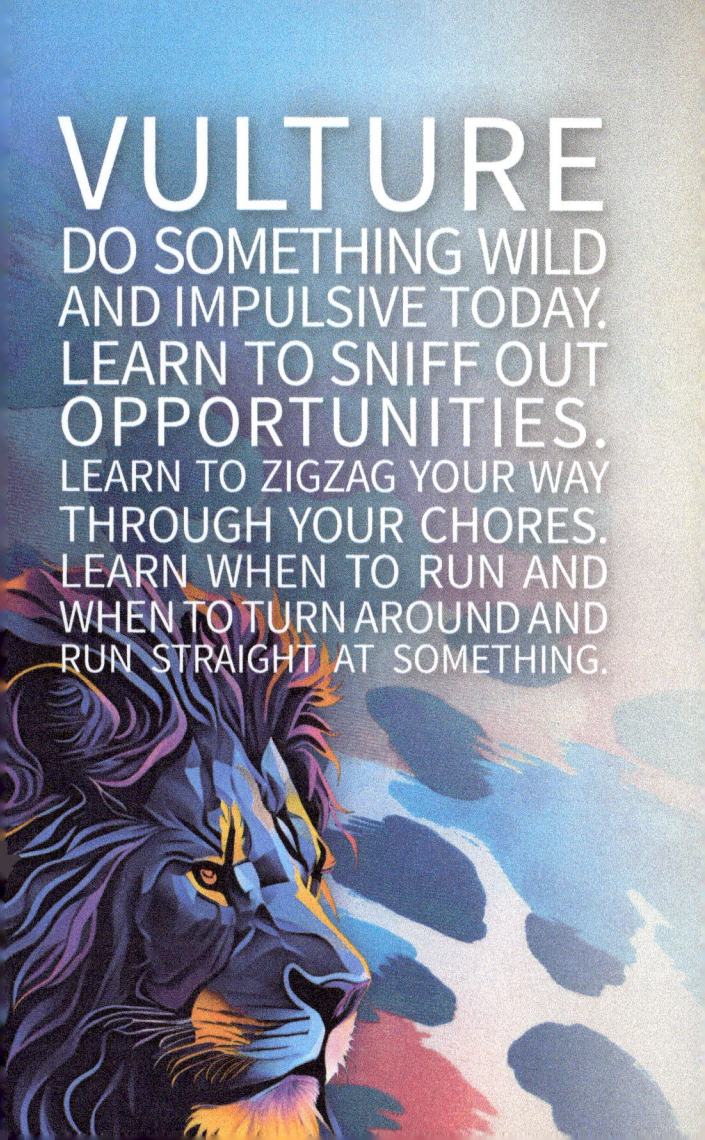

PRAYING MANTIS

Pray, pray, pray! Do not think of it as the standard prayer - but a conversation with up above co-creating what you want in your life. Then see it as so and take action!!! Action means you are focused on it and are showing that you are willing to do what it takes. Allow the universe to help you or guide you towards something even better than you thought imaginable.

The animal kingdom is always speaking - we just have to listen.

When an animal crosses your path and you feel an unexplainable pull, trust that it's more than coincidence. It's a message.

Take a moment to pause, breathe, and ask: *What wisdom do you have for me?* You may receive a word, a vision, or a feeling deep in your soul. Sometimes, the message is clear; other times, it unfolds over time and you may want to journal on it. And if nothing comes?

A simple *thank you* acknowledges the connection and keeps the channel open.

The more you do this, the more the messages will come easier and easier.

Every encounter is a reminder that we are all woven into the great web of life.

Stay open, stay curious, and let the animals guide you.

About Me

Julia is an author, publisher, and the creative heart behind The Giving Deck. Her mission? To help people hit pause, tune into their inner wisdom, and remember that love - starting with yourself - is the real magic of life.

Through her books and playful card decks, she invites you to embrace your messy, beautiful humanity. After all, who said self-discovery couldn't come with a side of laughter?

When not writing or designing, she's wandering in nature with her dogs, chatting with her chooks and duck, or plotting her next chocolate break. Because connection, joy, and a little fresh air make everything better.

To everyone reading this

Let this be your permission to chase your passions. You don't need to only be doing your passion, or only working a job, be in a different business. Your heart and soul are big enough to do both! Don't ever give up what is calling from your soul just because you think it should be a certain way.

Explore your passions comfortably while having money coming in from a different avenue. Or not and go large. You, your heart, soul and body will know the right answer for you, but just go out and grab it with both hands, whatever you do. And remember your job/business is also being of service, no matter the capacity. Whatever you do is making an impact.

www.ingramcontent.com/pod-product-compliance
Lightning Source LLC
Chambersburg PA
CBHW061738070526
44585CB00024B/2729